SHARKS FOR KIDS

Scalloped hammerhead

SHARKS FOR KIDS

A JUNIOR SCIENTIST'S GUIDE
to Great Whites, Hammerheads, and Other Sharks in the Sea

JUNIOR SCIENTISTS

DAVID McGUIRE

ROCKRIDGE PRESS

This book is dedicated to my seventh-grade teacher, Dr. Floyd Siders, who inspired me to study marine biology, and my mother and father, Pat and Edward McGuire, who encouraged me to study and protect sharks and ocean life.

For general information on our other products and services or to obtain technical support, please contact our Customer Care Department within the United States at (866) 744-2665, or outside the United States at (510) 253-0500.

Rockridge Press publishes its books in a variety of electronic and print formats. Some content that appears in print may not be available in electronic books, and vice versa.

Interior and Cover Designer: Jami Spittler
Series Design: The Junior Scientists Team
Art Producer: Tom Hood
Editor: Mary Colgan
Production Manager: Michael Kay
Production Editor: Sigi Nacson

Illustrations Kate Francis ©2020, pp. 2, 4, 5, 8, 15, 16, 18, 20, 22, 25, 27; Kluva/Shutterstock, p. 23; Photography Mark Conlin/Alamy, cover; Tom McHugh/Science Source, pp. 18, 57; Wildestanimal/Alamy, pp. ii, 30, 31; Hubert Yann/Alamy, p. vi; SeaTops/Alamy, pp. viii, 1; Beara Creative/Alamy, pp. 11, 54; Duncan Murrell/Alamy, p. 28; lophius_sub/Alamy, p. 33; Gary Bell/OceanwideImages.com, p. 34; Mark Conlin/VWPics/Alamy, p. 35; Becca Saunders/Auscape/Minden Pictures, p. 37; Louise Murray/Alamy, p. 41; Andy Murch/Elasmodiver, pp. 42, 44, 46, 47, 53, 60, 70, 72; blinkwinkel/Alamy, p. 44; Felix Choo/Alamy, p. 48; Poelzer Wolfgang/Alamy, p. 49; Kelvin Aitken/VWPics/Alamy, pp. 51, 59; Jeffrey Rotman/Biosphoto/Minden Pictures, p. 52; Brad Leue/Alamy, pp. 55, 74; NOAA/Alamy, p. 58; ArteSub/Alamy, p. 62; Stocktrek Images/Science Source, p. 63; SPL/Science Source, p. 64; Gaertner/Alamy, p. 65; Joao Ponces/Alamy, p. 66; Jeffrey Rotman/Science Source, p. 68; Mark Boulton/Science Source, p. 69; Frederick R McConnaughey/Science Source, p. 71
Author Photograph courtesy of Gretchen Coffman

ISBN: Print 978-1-64739-757-9 | Ebook 978-1-64739-458-5
R1

Printed in China

CONTENTS

Blacktip reef sharks

WELCOME, JUNIOR SCIENTIST!

When you hear the word *shark*, what comes to your mind? Many people think sharks are scary, dangerous beasts that are just waiting to snap up unlucky swimmers. But when I hear the word *shark*, I think of incredible fish that come in hundreds of different shapes and live in every part of the ocean. I have dived with giant whale sharks and tiny dogfish. I am amazed every time. As a swimmer, surfer, and scientist, I live with sharks. When you are finished with this book, I hope you will be as excited about sharks as I am. Then, when you hear the word *shark*, you will think, *Sharks are cool!*

Caribbean reef sharks

PART ONE

REMARKABLE SHARKS

Let's go on an adventure under the sea—what sharks call home-sweet-home. You will learn that some sharks are as big as whales, while others can fit in your hand. Some have funny names, like crocodile sharks, goblin sharks, and catsharks. Some have long tails, some have noses like saws, while others have fins like an angel's wings. Right now, there are hundreds of **species**, or kinds, of sharks, but scientists discover new species every year. Are you ready? Let's dive in!

What Is a Shark?

Sharks are a very special kind of fish. While most fish have bones like you and me, sharks don't. Their skeleton is made out of a rubbery material called cartilage. This is why they are called **cartilaginous fish**. You have cartilage, too. It forms your ears and nose and helps your joints move smoothly.

Without bones, sharks are lighter and more flexible than other fish. They have large muscles and fins that make them fast swimmers and excellent **predators**, or hunters. Not all sharks are giant creatures like whale sharks. Most species are less than three feet long. They eat anything from microscopic animals to dead whales. Like other fish, sharks breathe through gills. As you'll read, sharks can be many different shapes and sizes and have different ways of eating. All sharks are important for keeping the world's oceans healthy.

Sharks come in all sizes, from whale sharks that grow as large as 60 feet to the tiny dwarf lanternshark, which could fit on a page of this book.

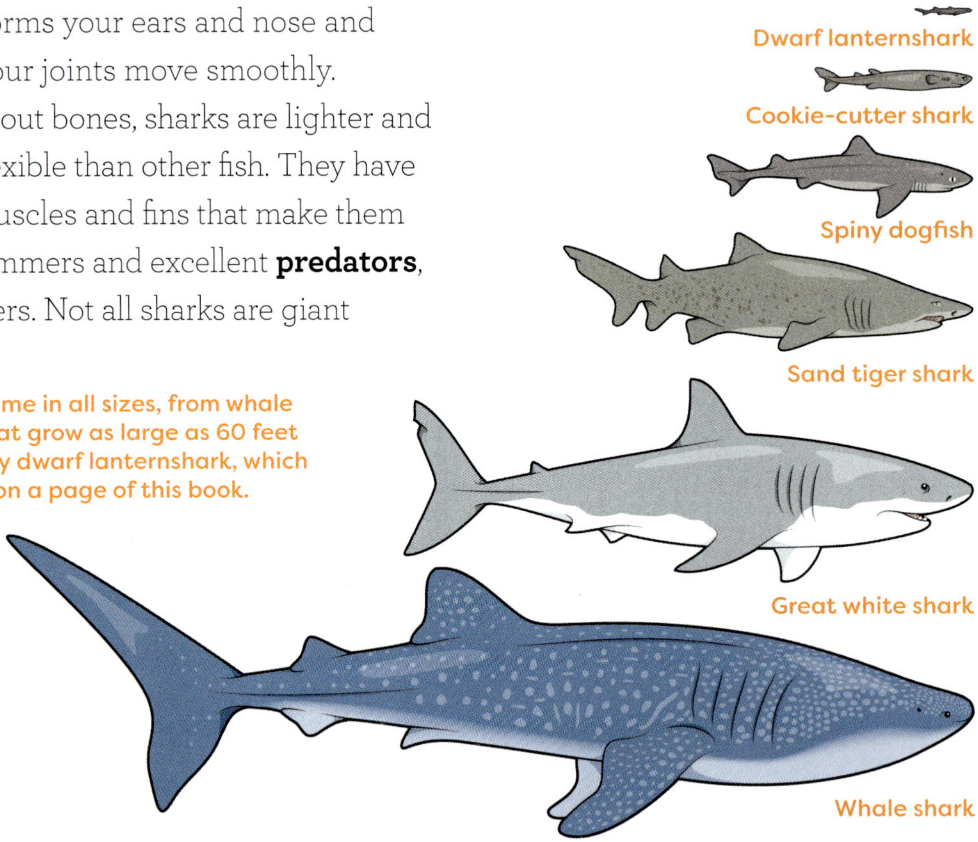

Sharks Past and Present

Sharks have been around for hundreds of millions of years. That's not easy to do! Sharks' bodies have **evolved**, or changed, over time, to be able to live in all parts of the world's oceans. Today they are found everywhere from the freezing waters of the deep sea to the warm, shallow waters of the tropics.

Since sharks don't have bones, they usually don't leave behind good **fossils**. The cartilage skeleton disintegrates, or breaks into small pieces, over time. But ancient sharks have left some things behind—their hardened teeth, and scales. These things give scientists clues to help solve the mystery of ancient sharks.

Scientists discovered a fossil in Canada that could be an ancestor to sharks and fish with bones, like tuna. It was from the Acanthodian group—a type of "spiny shark" called *Doliodus problematicus*. Scientists believe that some of these **extinct** fish lived more than 400 million years ago. Just imagine, these ancient sharks swam in the ocean long before Earth had trees!

Scientists have found shark fossils in Kentucky, which is in the middle of the United States. How did the sharks get there? North America was covered by a shallow sea about 360 million years ago! One of the ancient sharks found there is *Cladoselache*. It was only about three feet long and had teeth that looked like forks with three prongs!

Sharks were slowly filling the world's oceans. Around 359 to 299 million years ago, the number of sharks went way up. Some scientists call it the "golden age of sharks." Fossils of many species have been left behind from this period. Some of them may have looked a little weird to us. *Helicoprion* had teeth like a buzz saw, and *Stethacanthus* had a large anvil-shaped fin on its back.

Earth's climate changed, and around 250 million years ago, 95 percent of the living things—including sharks—on Earth went extinct. This is called the Permian extinction. It was the largest extinction in our planet's history. After an event like this, new species evolved to adapt to the world left behind. The sharks we know today, called modern sharks, came on the scene about 100 million years ago.

There have been many shark ancestors, but none are as famous as the megalodon. This giant shark may have grown to 65 feet and weighed over 100 tons. That is much longer than a school bus and heavier than 16 elephants! Scientists have found only jaws and teeth from megalodon. This amazing creature went extinct about 2.6 million years ago. It is very unlikely these sharks still lurk far beneath the ocean's surface, but one can always hope!

Acanthodian shark

The Shark Family

You may have heard of great white sharks, which scientists and shark experts usually call white sharks. Some people call these sharks white pointers, but they are the same species. *White shark* and *white pointer* are both common names for this type of shark. Common names are kind of like nicknames and can be confusing. Let's introduce you to sharks by their real names, using a scientific system called **taxonomy**.

Taxonomy is a way of naming every living creature on Earth. All animals belong to the kingdom Animalia (including sharks and us humans). The Animalia kingdom splits into smaller and smaller groups of creatures that look and act a lot like one another. Every living creature has seven groups it belongs to: kingdom, phylum, class, order, family, genus, and species.

Most of the time, scientists call living things by their genus and species names. Humans are called *Homo sapiens*. A great white shark is called *Carcharodon carcharias*. Today, scientists know there are about 500 species of living sharks. There are eight orders of sharks. On the right, you can see one type of shark from each order. Let's learn about them!

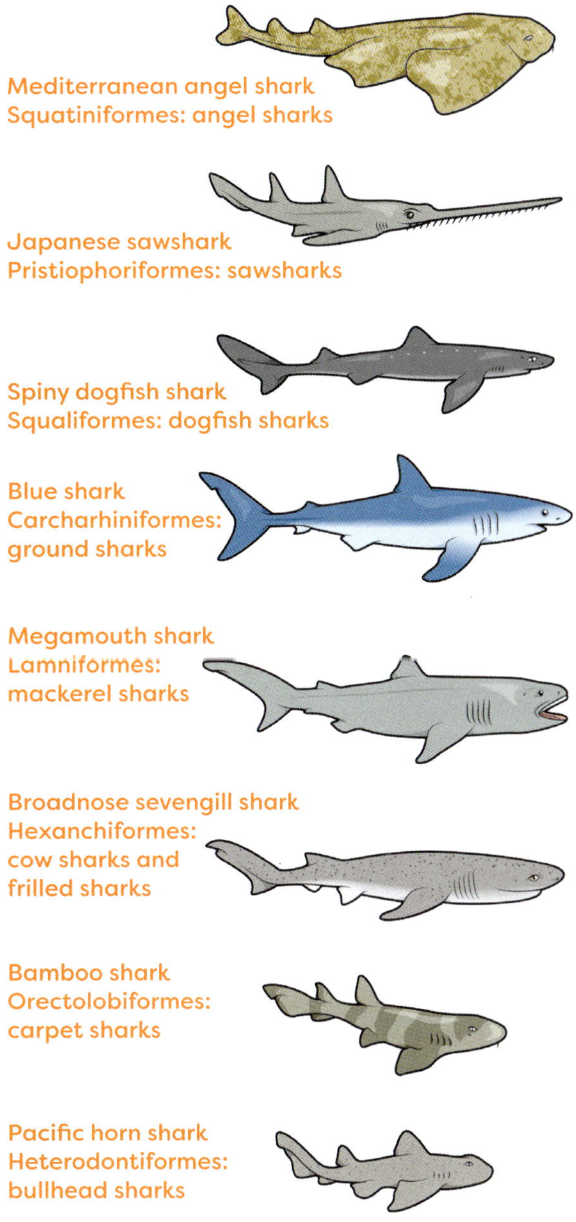

OCEAN ZONES IN A JAR

Have you ever felt a hot side-walk on a sunny day? Just like the sun warms the ground, it also warms the water in the ocean. But the ocean is very deep. The sun cannot reach all the way to the bottom. There are five zones in the ocean, starting with the surface, where there is light and the water is warm. As the ocean gets deeper, there is less sunlight in each zone. The water becomes colder and darker. Let's explore the zones of the ocean!

What you'll need:

- **3 PAPER CUPS**
- **A LARGE JAR**
- **CORN SYRUP**
- **BLACK AND BLUE FOOD COLORINGS**
- **DISH SOAP**
- **VEGETABLE OIL**
- **RUBBING ALCOHOL**

1. Begin by making the trench zone, the deepest zone of the ocean. In a paper cup, mix ¾ cup corn syrup with black food coloring. Then pour this into your jar.

2. Next comes the abyss zone. There is no light or oxygen here, but some creatures, like sea stars and squid, make the abyss their home. For this zone, slowly pour ¾ cup dish soap on top of the corn syrup.

3. The midnight zone is completely dark, but many creatures live there. Some whales even visit this zone to hunt. To make your midnight zone, pour ¾ cup water into a paper cup and mix in the dark blue food coloring. Carefully pour this into your jar.

4. The twilight zone is still beyond the reach of full sunlight. Some fish in this zone are bioluminescent, which means they make their own light! To create your twilight zone, slowly pour ¾ cup vegetable oil into your jar.

5. The top zone of the ocean is the sunlight zone. This is where coral reefs and ocean plants are found. In a paper cup, mix ¾ cup rubbing alcohol with light blue food coloring and pour this mixture into your jar.

And now you have your very own ocean in a jar!

Sharks Jaws to Tail

So, what makes a shark a shark? What cool features help them swim, hunt, and eat? In this chapter, you will find out how sharks are built to be perfect predators in the water.

SKELETON

A shark's cartilage skeleton is light and flexible, or "bendy." This helps sharks swim fast and with less effort. The backbone, or spine, is also very flexible. It contains many more little bones, called vertebrae, than the spines of most other animals. Humans have 33 vertebrae, blue whales have 64, and white sharks have 133. This makes them as whippy as a garden hose!

JAWS

The upper jaw of many of the larger sharks is not attached to their skulls. This lets them take giant bites. What about teeth? Some sharks have

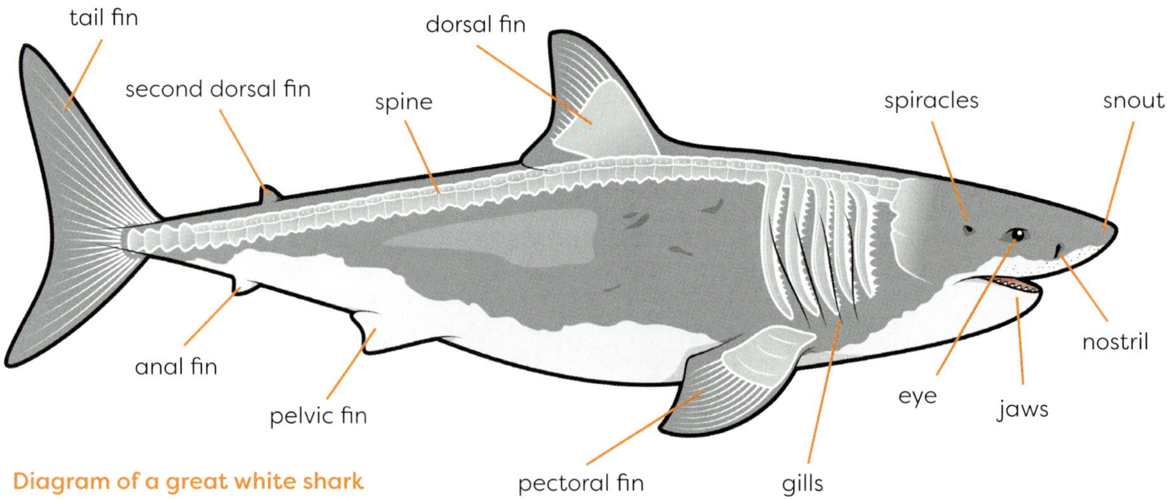

Diagram of a great white shark

hundreds of teeth in their mouths at one time! The teeth are replaced as they wear out. Some sharks go through 30,000 teeth in their lifetime!

SNOUT

Shark snouts, or noses, can be round, pointy, or flat. Look closely at a shark snout, and you will see tiny black dots. They are little holes, or pores, called **ampullae of Lorenzini**. Sharks can detect tiny amounts of electricity through these pores.

SPIRACLES AND GILLS

Sharks get the oxygen they need from the water using their gills. As they swim, water flows past the gills and little blood vessels pick up oxygen. Most sharks have five gills on each side, but some species have six or seven. Some sharks also have **spiracles**. Spiracles are small holes behind a shark's eyes that pump water past their gills. This lets many species of sharks rest on the bottom while still being able to breathe.

EYES

Shark eyes don't work quite as well as yours do. They are best at seeing light against dark, called contrast, very well. Sharks have eyelids, but they don't blink. The eyelids are only used to protect their eyes during a fight or when eating. Some sharks have something called a **nictitating membrane**. This is a thin "skin" that rolls over the eye and protects it when the shark feeds. Some sharks, like the great white, don't have eyelids at all and roll their eyes back when feeding.

NOSTRILS

Did you know sharks have nostrils? They do! They are not used for breathing like ours, but they are used for smelling. Sharks have two sets of nostrils, called nares. Water flows into one pair and exits out the other pair. Some sharks have pieces of skin that look like tassels around their noses. Scientists believe the sharks use them like feelers to help them find **prey**.

FINS

Like all fish, sharks have fins. They are made of cartilage. Dorsal fins keep the shark from rolling over while swimming. Most sharks have two. Some sharks, like the spiny dogfish, have spines in front of their dorsal fins. They are good protection against predators.

Pectoral fins move the shark up and down in the water and help it steer. Some sharks also have anal fins for the same purpose. Finally, the tail fin is what pushes the shark forward. All of these fins come in many shapes and sizes, depending on the species.

SKIN

Fish are covered in scales. Sharks are no different, but the type of scales they have is! Shark scales are called **dermal denticles**. They are like tiny teeth! The word *dermal* means “skin” and *denticle* means “small tooth.” These scales are hard, pointed, and overlap each other. Water moves easily over the denticles, which means it takes the shark less energy to swim. Parasites, which are harmful to sharks, have a hard time attaching to the scales. So, it is almost like the shark is wearing a coat of armor!

MUSCLE

It takes muscle power to move quickly through the water. Fast-swimming sharks have two types of muscles for this: red muscle and white muscle. Red muscle is used when the shark is cruising along at a relaxed pace. White muscle is for quick bursts of speed.

DIVE DEEPER

Sharks that are strong swimmers have tails with a larger upper part and smaller lower part. These parts are called lobes. Thresher sharks have the longest tails of all the sharks. The long upper lobe is almost as long as the shark itself! To hunt, the thresher swims through a school of fish. It snaps its tail like a whip. This quick movement can smack or stun fish nearby. Then all the thresher needs to do is circle around to eat its supper!

Thresher shark

Shark Senses

You use your senses every day to explore and understand the world around you. Smelling a bear or hearing it growl in the woods warns us that danger could be nearby and we should leave the area. Humans have five senses: smell, touch, taste, sight, and hearing. Sharks have the same five senses we have, and one we don't. It's called **electroreception**. Let's take a look at what makes sharks so special in the animal kingdom.

SEEING UNDER THE SEA

How well do sharks see? Most species have excellent vision but do not see in color like you and me, and not all sharks see things the same way. How well and what a shark sees depends on where it lives and how it hunts. Some sharks that live in deep water, like prickly sharks, have eyes that are very sensitive to even small amounts of light. Other deep-water sharks, like the goblin shark, have small eyes and bad eyesight.

Mako sharks have large eyes with excellent vision to track fast-swimming prey like tuna and sailfish. Hammerhead sharks have an eye at each end of their hammer-shaped heads. They can actually see behind themselves!

SHARK BITE

Port Jackson sharks have black stripes beneath their eyes. Scientists think this helps reduce sun glare—like the grease football players use!

THE NOSE KNOWS

Smell is one of the most important senses to sharks. In fact, about two-thirds of the shark's brain by weight is used for figuring out what the shark is actually smelling. Sharks can smell very small amounts of chemicals in the water. For example, a lemon shark's nose is so sensitive that it can detect one teaspoon of blood in a large swimming pool.

A shark can also tell where a scent is coming from. If a scent is stronger on the left, it is detected by the left side of the brain. When a shark swims in an S-shaped pattern, it can track a "stream" of odor. As it moves back and forth, it focuses in on areas where the scent is the strongest.

HEARING THINGS

You've probably noticed that sharks don't have ears you can see like sea lions and humans. If they did, the ears would probably flap in the current and slow them down! Shark ears are two holes just behind the eyes. They are excellent at hearing very low sounds.

Sharks can hear tones that are ten times lower than the lowest key on the piano. Wounded animals that are struggling make these types of sounds in the water. To a shark, it might sound like the dinner bell! Sound travels four times faster in water than air, so sharks hear things that are far away more quickly than we can—sometimes from miles away. Like humans' ears, sharks' ears also help them with balance.

FEELING LIKE A SHARK

Just like you, a shark can tell when something touches its skin. But it has other ways of "feeling" what is around it. Sharks have an organ that runs from snout to tail along their sides called the **lateral line**. This organ is made of tubes connected to nerve cells that feel the movements made by struggling fish or an approaching predator. This lets the shark hunt even when it's completely dark!

Since sharks do not have hands, they use their mouths to check out objects that might be interesting to eat. Tiger sharks are known for mouthing objects they are curious about. They've even swallowed odd items like license plates, bottles, and tires! Some sharks, like angel sharks and bullhead sharks, have tiny "whiskers" called **barbels** near the front of their mouths. These barbels are used to sense prey.

> **SHARK BITE**
> Many sharks become paralyzed for several minutes when turned upside down. This is called tonic immobility.

TASTE TEST

Sharks don't need a sense of taste to detect prey, so it may be the least important sense a shark has. Sharks don't have tongues like humans do, but they do have taste buds located near their teeth. These taste buds are likely used to find out if something is actually food or not. Many sharks are very picky about what they eat. The white shark's favorite meal is elephant seal because it has a lot of fat. Fat is high in calories—which gives these strong-swimming sharks the energy they need to survive.

Sometimes a shark makes a mistake and bites a human or a sea otter, thinking they are its usual prey—a nice, fat seal! In many cases, the shark mouths the human and spits it out with little harm. The wounded sea otter usually dies when this happens, but the shark doesn't eat it. Sea otters don't have much fat, so they aren't a good food source. The shark moves on to find a better meal.

SUPER SENSE

Let's talk about the sense you and I don't have: electroreception. Earlier you learned that a shark's snout has hundreds of ampullae of Lorenzini on it. These pores are connected to thin tubes filled with a gel. The gel detects electricity and sends a message through a nerve to the brain: "There is food nearby!"

Living things send out tiny electrical signals. When a creature's heart beats, it makes a small electrical pulse. Sharks can detect a heartbeat from several feet away. The hammerhead shark's wide, flat head is covered in ampullae. It moves its head back and forth over the sandy bottom like a metal detector searching for unseen coins. This helps the shark find stingrays or flounder hidden in the sand. This extra sense also helps sharks find their prey at night or in the deep sea where there is no sunlight.

SHARK BITE
Engineers have discovered crocodile sharks chewing on communication cables in the deep sea. They were probably attracted to the electrical field.

This illustration shows how far some sharks' senses can reach. Sharks can smell blood in water from as far away as a quarter mile.

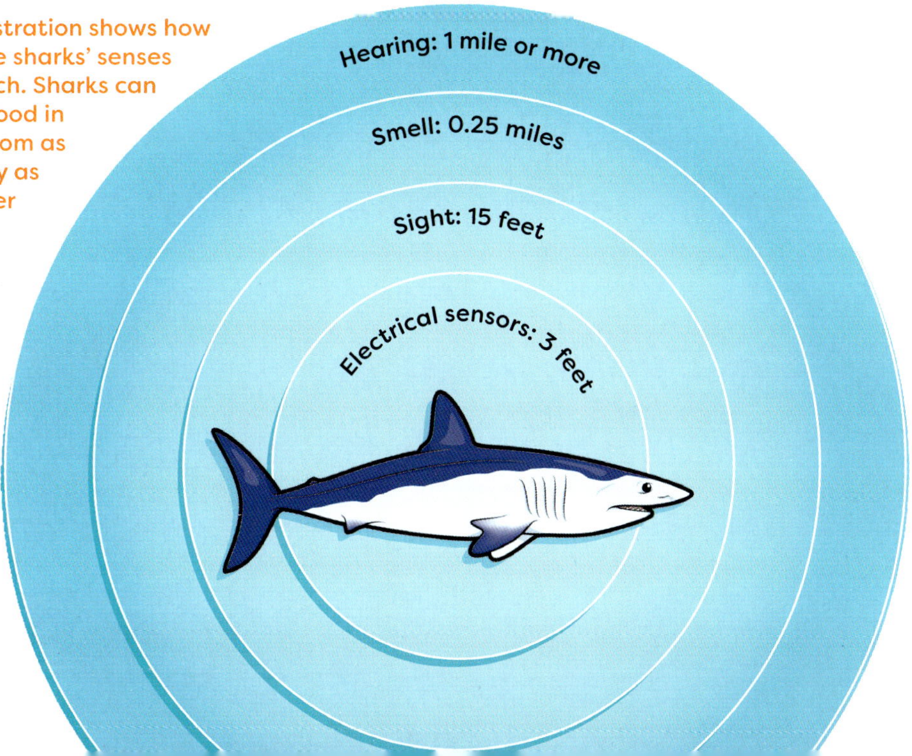

Baby Sharks

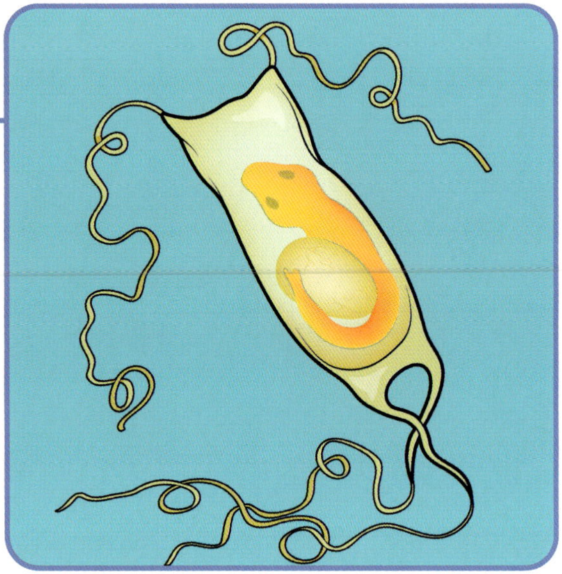

Shark egg case

Where do baby sharks come from? Do they hatch from eggs? Are they born alive? The answer is yes—and yes! Shark babies, called pups, are born three different ways. Some sharks, like the horn shark, lay eggs. The eggs have a tough casing that protects the developing baby shark, called an embryo, from harm. The embryo is fed by a yolk—like the one you'd find in a chicken egg. When the pup is finished growing, it chews its way out and swims off.

Other sharks give birth to live babies. There are two different ways these babies grow inside the mother. One is the same way human babies form. The baby sharks develop inside the mother shark and get nutrients from her body through an umbilical cord. Depending on the species, most babies grow for nine to twelve months in the womb. Some dogfish take three years! The pups are born alive and swim away right after being born.

SHARK BITE

When baby sawsharks are born, their teeth are folded so they don't hurt their mother during birth. The pups look like tiny versions of the adults.

Most shark babies develop the other way inside their mother. Instead of laying eggs, the mother shark keeps the eggs inside her body. The eggs hatch inside the mother. The first babies to hatch eat the other eggs. In some species, such as tiger sharks, the unborn pups will even eat their smaller brothers and sisters! This means only the strongest babies are born.

Once they are born, baby sharks are on their own. Their mothers do not take care of them. In fact, sometimes if the babies don't swim away fast enough, the mother might eat them!

SHARK BITE
Greenland sharks can't start having babies until they are more than 150 years old!

A Shark's Life

After a pup is born, then what? Unlike human babies, shark pups can do everything their parents do as soon as they are born. The first goal in a young shark's life is to eat and avoid being eaten! What happens from there is different for each species of shark.

Let's follow a blacktip reef shark through its life. Blacktips grow inside their mothers for 9 to 16 months. The pups are born tail first. They wiggle free from their mother and swim quickly to the bottom to find a hiding place. They are about one to two feet long when born.

The young sharks have a mouthful of teeth—perfect for munching crabs, clams, octopuses, and small fish. Young blacktips stay in shallow reefs and lagoons to hide from other sharks and predators. Once they become adults, the sharks can safely travel to deeper water, where larger fish live. There, they hunt stingrays and schools of fish—often together in groups, or packs. These sharks are social, which means they like being around other sharks.

Blacktip reef sharks grow to be between five and six feet long—about as long as an adult human is tall. They weigh about 275 pounds, which is about twice what a human woman weighs. Male sharks start looking for mates when they are 4 years old. Females are ready to mate when they are about 7. Scientists believe these sharks live 10 to 13 years, maybe longer.

Blacktip reef sharks live on coral reefs in tropical and subtropical oceans.

Blacktip reef shark

WATCH SHARKS LIVE!

Would you like to see some of the sharks in this book in action? Some aquariums have shark cams so you can watch sharks live online.

MONTEREY BAY AQUARIUM'S SHARK CAM

MontereyBayAquarium.org

Watch as bat rays, sevengill sharks, leopard sharks, and spiny dogfish swim past. How many sharks can you identify? Try looking for a camouflaged Pacific angel shark!

AQUARIUM OF THE PACIFIC'S SHARK LAGOON CAM

AquariumofPacific.org

Travel to the tropics to see blacktip and gray reef sharks, giant stingrays, and even zebra sharks. Watch the different swimming patterns and find different shark tail shapes. Can you see how the sharks use their tails to push them forward?

Leopard shark

Shark Talk

How do sharks tell other sharks what they are thinking? Many ocean creatures communicate, or talk to each other, with sound. Humpback whales sing. Dolphins click and squeak. But, other than the clacking of their teeth while feeding, almost all sharks are silent.

This doesn't mean sharks don't have something to say! Sharks communicate in other ways. A group of hammerhead sharks, called a shiver, communicate with each other by moving their bodies. When danger is near, these sharks shake their heads and bodies to alert their schoolmates. Usually, these sharks swim with a slow S-shaped motion, like snakes. Swell sharks respond to danger by gulping water and swelling up to almost twice their normal size. It is hard to eat a swell shark that has wedged itself into a crack and puffed up to make a tight fit. When the shark gets rid

Some sharks will arch their backs and drop their pectoral fins to warn other animals to stay away.

of all the water it gulped, it sounds like it's barking!

Some sharks, like gray reef sharks, arch their backs and point their pectoral fins down. This is a warning to anyone around that means, "Stay away!" I saw this while diving with reef sharks in the South Pacific. At first the sharks were peaceful. Then there was a switch. The sharks sent a clear message that it was time for us to leave. We did!

SHARK BITE
Great white sharks threaten others of their kind by slapping their tails on the water. This sometimes happens when one shark gets too close to another great white's lunch!

Not all sharks want to be around other sharks all the time. But even those sharks spend some time with other members of their species. Some species **migrate**, or travel, long distances in groups. Other sharks live with other members during breeding time, then break into small groups for the rest of the year. Many sharks, like goblin sharks, live alone until it is time to mate. Scientists think these sharks find each other by sniffing **pheromones** in the water.

SHARK BITE
The word *shark* may have come from the German word *Schurke*, which means "villain" or "scoundrel."

Sharks on the Hunt

Sharks are predators, but do they all hunt and eat the same way? Nope! Let's explore the different ways sharks feed themselves. Whale sharks have tiny little teeth but don't use them to eat. Instead, they use their gills to strain out tiny plants and animals called plankton. These gentle sharks swim with their mouths open. The water goes into their mouths and is strained by their gills on the way out. Only the plankton is left for the whale shark to swallow.

Mako sharks quickly charge at fast-swimming fish like tuna and snap them up. Tiger sharks sometimes circle around and bump their prey before attacking. Some scientists think they do this to size up their dinner. Goblin sharks hunt in the dark using their long, ampullae-covered snouts to detect their prey. Their jaws shoot out lightning fast to grab lunch. Their teeth are pointed backward, which makes it difficult for prey to get out of the shark's grasp.

Dogfish hunt in packs and herd fish together before snapping them up. A pack of dogfish, called a swarm, can have thousands of sharks! Greenland sharks will eat dead animals like whales. Two men in Newfoundland were surprised to find a Greenland shark that had a large piece of moose in its mouth. The shark was stranded halfway out of the water!

Whale sharks eat as much as 46 pounds of plankton a day.

DIVE DEEPER

Great white sharks are silent hunters that look for seals swimming at the surface. The seals' shape is easy to see against the bright sky. These sharks charge and bite their prey. This is called **ambush predation**. The sharks usually bite and spit their prey out while circling it before eating the weakened animal (which can bite back). Sometimes a surfer or swimmer is the victim of this "bite and spit" behavior. Most of the time, these sharks realize we are not their favorite fatty meal and do not come in for a second bite.

Sharks Around the World

Where do sharks live? All over our planet! They live in all five oceans, and a few even cruise lakes and rivers! In the ocean, sharks live at all depths. Where a shark lives depends on what it needs to survive. Angel sharks live around the world in all **temperate** and **tropical** oceans. They like shallow water and soft ocean floors. They have large mouths that suck fish and crabs out of the sand, so they usually stay on the ocean floor.

SHARK BITE

Scientists have recently figured out that shark teeth evolved from the same cells that form taste buds!

Frilled sharks live in deep water, 150 to 3,000 feet below the surface. They live in the Atlantic and Pacific oceans and spend most of their time in the deeper areas. Scientists believe they migrate upward from the deep at night to chase their prey: squid. These sharks have eyes that are very sensitive to light to help them hunt.

The kitefin shark is a type of dogfish. It lives near the bottom, between 600 and 2,000 feet. These sharks eat almost anything, including fish, squid, clams, mussels, and crabs. They use their sharp cutting teeth to take bites out of whales and porpoises, too. They live around the world in warm patches of water.

The megamouth shark is a large shark with rubbery lips and tiny teeth that feeds on microscopic creatures called plankton. This shark lives in a band around the world in tropical and temperate seas. Fewer than 100 of these mysterious sharks have been seen in the wild. Some megamouths have dived to 15,000 feet, but they also hang out in shallower waters. Like the frilled shark, megamouths also migrate upward at night.

Oceanic whitetip sharks are found all over the world. They mostly live in the tropical and subtropical waters of the Pacific, Atlantic, and Indian Oceans, as shown in this map.

HOW DO SHARKS FLOAT?

Whale sharks, the biggest sharks in the sea, weigh about 40,000 pounds on average. That's as much as five Asian elephants stacked on top of one another! So how does an animal that huge keep from sinking to the bottom of the ocean? There are three things that help sharks float: the shape of their fins; their cartilage, which weighs less than bones; and their oil-filled livers. This simple experiment demonstrates how sharks' oil-filled livers keep them afloat.

What you'll need:

- **TWO WATER BOTTLES OF THE SAME SIZE**
- **WATER**
- **VEGETABLE OIL**
- **BUCKET**

1. Fill the bucket with enough water to cover your water bottles.
2. Fill one water bottle with water and the other with vegetable oil.
3. One at a time, place your two bottles in the bucket.

Which one floats? If you like, you can decorate the oil-filled bottle with markers or paint to make a shark toy.

Shark Conservation

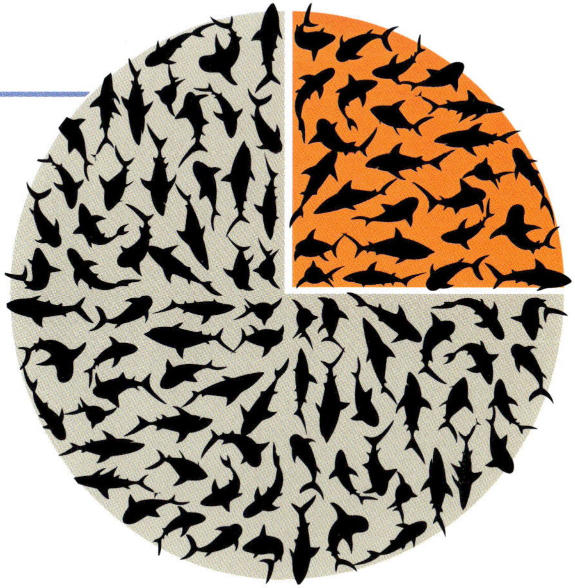

Twenty-five percent of sharks and rays are in danger of extinction.

As we learned, sharks have survived for hundreds of millions of years. But these days, sharks are disappearing from the world's oceans. The biggest threat to sharks is us—people. Humans kill sharks for food, and in huge numbers. Pollution and **habitat** loss are also things that are making it hard for sharks to live and grow.

Scientists estimate that more than 100 million sharks are killed each year, and most of these, like the oceanic whitetip, blue, and mako, are killed for their fins. The fins are used for shark fin soup—a very popular dish in Asia. Sharks take a long time to reproduce, or make new sharks. They are being killed faster than they can reproduce, so their numbers are going down. Almost seven million sharks each year are also caught accidentally in fishing nets and die.

You probably have heard that Earth is heating up. This is called global warming, and it is forcing many fish to move in order to survive. The sharks follow their food and end up in places where they risk running into humans who will fish them up. The ocean's water is changing, too. Pollution is making it harder for shark babies to survive. It is also affecting sharks' sense of smell, which they need to hunt. Changing water chemistry also affects sharks' prey, so it's harder for sharks to find food.

Between overfishing, global warming, and pollution, 25 percent of all sharks and rays are in danger of going extinct. It doesn't help that sharks aren't as cute and cuddly as panda bears or lions. People tend to be less likely to help animals they are afraid of.

But there is hope. Killing sharks for their fins is now illegal in most countries. Countries all over the world are working to cut down on shark fishing. This is already helping in some areas. Groups have also created refuge areas and no-fishing zones that protect some sharks and other animals and where they live. Most of all, young people are learning that sharks are important and are joining in to save them. Hopefully, you will be one of them!

Whale sharks

DIVE DEEPER

If you've ever worn goggles while swimming in water that isn't crystal clear, you know how hard it can be to see underwater. Human eyes are designed to see in air. Shark eyes, of course, are designed to see in water. But how can they see even in deep, dark, murky water hundreds of feet below the surface? Sharks can see in very low light because of a layer of cells located behind the retina (the part of the eye that senses light). This layer is called the *tapetum lucidum*. It is made of mirrored crystals. When light hits the crystals, it reflects back onto the retina. This causes sharks' eyes to shine green when observed with a light. The same thing happens with cats' and dogs' eyes when a light is shined on them in the dark. This is because cats and dogs have a tapetum lucidum, too! Who would have guessed your furry friends have something in common with a shark?

Oceanic blacktip sharks

PART TWO

SHARKS UP CLOSE

Are you ready to meet some sharks up close and personal? Earlier you learned about taxonomy. We are going to learn about sharks by grouping them into their orders. There are eight orders (or groups) of sharks. The sharks in each order have things in common, like body shape and habits. We will begin with the bottom-dwelling angel sharks.

Squatiniformes: Angel Sharks

Angel sharks have a very small family. There is only one family of sharks in their order (most orders of sharks have at least two families). Squatiniformes have been around for about 150 million years. The 24 species of angel sharks are **benthic**. This means they live on the ocean bottom in shallow water and deep water to 4,000 feet.

Angel sharks are flat and wide. Their pectoral fins are held out to the sides and look like angel's wings. They have two dorsal fins. Their tail fin has a small upper lobe and long lower lobe. This is different from most sharks, whose tails are the opposite. Look inside an angel shark's mouth and you will see several rows of pointed triangle-shaped teeth on the top and bottom. There is a gap with no teeth in the center bottom. This is helpful when grasping prey. These sharks have barbels on their noses.

Most angel sharks grow to about five feet long. Angel sharks around the world have similar shapes, life histories, and diets. These sharks spend most of their day hidden in the mud or sand. They are nocturnal, which means they are active and hunt at night. All species have camouflage skin and are excellent ambush predators. Their skin is gray, green, or white and has spots to blend in with the mud or sand.

Where in the world can you find angel sharks? Look for them in tropical and warm temperate waters along the edges of the continents in the Atlantic, Pacific, and Indian oceans. They also live in the Mediterranean Sea. Angel shark mothers carry their eggs for 10 months inside their bodies and give birth to 2 to 25 pups. Angel sharks live where humans live, so they are often fished for food. Unfortunately, they have been overfished in most of the places where they live.

Mediterranean Angel Shark

Squatina squatina

SAY IT! *"skwah-TEE-nah skwah-TEE-nah"*

The Mediterranean angel shark uses its large fins to bury itself in sand to wait for prey. Only its eyes are visible. When a fish comes close, the shark uses its tail to spring up and snatch its prey. This shark is also called a monkfish because the shape of its fins makes it look like the shark is wearing a monk's hood.

SHARK STATS

COMMON NAME: Mediterranean angel shark

SCIENTIFIC NAME: *Squatina squatina*

WHERE IT'S FOUND: Soft bottoms in mud and sand; the northeast Atlantic from Norway to northwest Africa, the Canary Islands, the Black Sea, and the Mediterranean Sea

SIZE: 6 to 7.3 feet

DIET: Flatfishes like flounder, skates, crabs, clams, octopuses, squid

LIFE SPAN: About 25 to 35 years

Australian Angel Shark

Squatina australis

SAY IT! *"skwah-TEE-nah aw-STRA-lis"*

Many angel sharks breathe by pumping water over their gills through their throats. But the Australian angel shark has gill flaps on the sides of its body, making this shark almost impossible to see while it lies camouflaged on the sandy seabed. During the day, this shark is still until a fish swims past. Then, it lunges and sucks its prey into its mouth like a vacuum cleaner.

SHARK STATS

COMMON NAME: Australian angel shark

SCIENTIFIC NAME: *Squatina australis*

WHERE IT'S FOUND: Soft bottoms in mud or sand and in seagrass beds; South and Western Australia, New South Wales, Tasmania, Victoria

SIZE: Up to 5 feet

DIET: Small fish, crabs, octopuses, and squid

LIFE SPAN: Unknown

Pacific Angel Shark

Squatina californica

SAY IT! *"skwah-TEE-nah ka-lih-FOR-nih-kah"*

How long are you willing to wait for food? The Pacific angel shark is very patient when it comes to hunting. It may stay buried in one spot for days—especially if the area is a good hunting ground. Eyesight is important for these sharks. Scientists believe they use sight more than any other sense to catch prey.

SHARK STATS

COMMON NAME: Pacific angel shark

SCIENTIFIC NAME: *Squatina californica*

WHERE IT'S FOUND: Soft bottoms in river mouths, rocky reefs, and kelp beds down to 300 feet

SIZE: Up to 5 feet

DIET: Fish, crabs, octopuses, and squid

LIFE SPAN: About 22 to 35 years

Pristiophoriformes: Sawsharks

It's easy to identify sharks from the Pristiophoriformes order. Just look for the ones that look like they have chain saws for noses! These unusual sharks are called sawsharks because of their long sawlike snouts. Sawsharks have slender, flat bodies with two triangular dorsal fins. They have large pectoral fins that they use to rest on the bottom, and a small tail fin. There are 10 species of sharks in this group.

The sawshark's amazing snout is lined with ampullae of Lorenzini. Depending on the species, it has as many as 48 sharp teeth that stick out from both sides. Two barbels hang like a drooping mustache halfway down the saw. The sawshark "stands" on its pectoral fins with its barbels dangling. When it senses a fish or squid, the shark slashes its head back and forth to kill its prey.

Sawsharks come in different colors, depending on the species. They can be a yellowish brown, pale to dark brown, or gray with light patterns. They have white bellies. Most have five gills but one genus has six. Sawfish are a type of ray, like a stingray, that lives on the bottom, too. You can tell sawsharks from sawfish because the sawsharks' gills are on the sides of their heads, not underneath like the sawfish.

You can find these sharks at the edges of most continents. They hang out in water that is 100 to 3,000 feet deep. They are not strong swimmers. Mother sharks give birth to 7 to 17 pups after carrying the eggs for about a year.

SHARK BITE

Many sawsharks live in deep water and extreme places. We know very little about their biology, and they are nearly impossible to photograph!

Longnose sawshark

Sixgill Sawshark

Pliotrema warreni

SAY IT! *"pli-oh-TREE-mah WAR-ren"*

For a while, scientists believed this shark was the only species in its genus. In 2019, two new sixgill sawsharks were found! This species has an interesting pattern of teeth. Each pair of long teeth has three smaller teeth between them.

SHARK STATS
COMMON NAME: Sixgill sawshark
SCIENTIFIC NAME: *Pliotrema warreni*
WHERE IT'S FOUND: Ocean bottom, along the **continental shelf** from 200 feet to 1,400 feet
SIZE: 3 to 5.5 feet
DIET: Fish, shrimp, and squid
LIFE SPAN: Unknown

Japanese Sawshark

Pristiophorus japonicus

SAY IT! *"pris-tee-oh-FOR-us juh-POH-ni-kus"*

Most things about the Japanese sawshark are still a mystery. It is not a common shark, so scientists really don't know how many are left or its full range. Unfortunately, this shark's toothy snout easily gets stuck in fishing nets meant for other fish. Many die this way.

SHARK STATS
COMMON NAME: Japanese sawshark
SCIENTIFIC NAME: *Pristiophorus japonicus*
WHERE IT'S FOUND: Ocean bottom in deep water along the continental shelf from 165 feet to 2,640 feet
SIZE: 4 to 6 feet
DIET: Fish, shrimp, and squid
LIFE SPAN: Unknown

Bahamas Sawshark

Pristiophorus schroederi

SAY IT! *"pris-tee-oh-FOR-us SHROH-deh-ree"*

Also called the American sawshark, this fish lives only around the islands of the Bahamas and in deeper areas off the east coast of southern Florida in the United States. It likes water that is 1,300 to 3,300 feet deep.

SHARK STATS

COMMON NAME: Bahamas sawshark

SCIENTIFIC NAME: *Pristiophorus schroederi*

WHERE IT'S FOUND: Tropical waters in the west Atlantic, ocean bottom in deep water

SIZE: 3 feet

DIET: Fish, shrimp, and crabs

LIFE SPAN: Unknown

African Dwarf Sawshark

Pristiophorus nancyae

SAY IT! *"pris-tee-oh-FOR-us nan-see-EE"*

The African dwarf sawshark is new to scientists. It was only discovered in 2011, when it was caught in a deep-sea fishing net in Mozambique. It is only two feet long, making it the smallest of the sawsharks. Its nose can be one-third of its entire body!

SHARK STATS

COMMON NAME: African dwarf sawshark

SCIENTIFIC NAME: *Pristiophorus nancyae*

WHERE IT'S FOUND: Open ocean in deeper waters of 930 to 1,870 feet

SIZE: Up to 2 feet

DIET: Shrimp

LIFE SPAN: Unknown

Squaliformes: Dogfish Sharks

These guys have been around for more than 153 million years! Over time, these ancient sharks have evolved into more than 120 species. They have five gills and two dorsal fins. Their dorsal fins are usually equipped with spines. They have large spiracles above and behind their big almond-shaped eyes. Some Squaliformes have body parts that glow! This order includes the oldest shark and the smallest shark known. The group has 10 families, including gulper sharks, sleeper sharks, and kitefin sharks. Do these names give you any clues about those sharks?

All dogfish sharks are predators, but they also are scavengers. This means they eat dead animals. Some, like the strange cookie-cutter shark, have special teeth that they use to chomp cookie-sized chunks of meat out of large prey. Even a white shark has been photographed with a cookie-cutter scar!

The Squaliformes live in all the world's oceans. Most species live on or near the bottom. Some live in deep open water. Others travel between both—like the lanternshark. During the day, this species lives in the deep. At night, it migrates up to shallower water to feed. Many species have special organs called photophores on their bellies. When a predator—or possible prey—looks up at a dogfish from deep water, the light on its belly matches the light coming from above and makes it hard to see.

Dogfish live a long time. Some live as long as 100 years, but that is nothing for the Greenland shark. It is the living vertebrate with the longest life span and may live as long as 400 years! Like most shark species, the mothers carry their eggs and then give birth. Much of the history of these sharks is unknown, so future shark scientists have a lot to learn and discover!

Greenland Shark

Somniosus microcephalus

SAY IT! *"sahm-nee-OH-sis my-kroh-SEF-ah-lus"*

The large Greenland shark belongs to the sleeper shark family. These sharks swim very slowly, which makes them seem sleepy. This deepwater shark prefers cold water and swims to depths of 4,000 feet. It even has a special chemical in its blood that acts like antifreeze. This chemical makes the Greenland shark's meat poisonous to eat.

SHARK STATS

COMMON NAME: Greenland shark

SCIENTIFIC NAME: *Somniosus microcephalus*

WHERE IT'S FOUND: Mostly in the northern Atlantic and Arctic, but also near the Antarctic; prefers swimming near the bottom

SIZE: Up to 24 feet

DIET: Many ocean creatures, including marine mammals and other sharks

LIFE SPAN: Between 300 and 500 years

Gulper Shark

Centrophorus granulosus

SAY IT! *"sen-troh-FOR-us gran-yoo-LOH-sus"*

The gulper shark, with its olive-gray skin and bright green eyes, is quite a mystery. Because gulper sharks live and eat near the bottom of the ocean, scientists still have a lot to learn about their habits. In some areas of the world, gulper sharks are endangered. People like to fish for these sharks because they have large livers—a part of their body used to make fish oil.

SHARK STATS

COMMON NAME: Gulper shark

SCIENTIFIC NAME: *Centrophorus granulosus*

WHERE IT'S FOUND: Deep waters near the west coast of Africa and southern Australia

SIZE: 5 feet

DIET: Bony fish, squid, and crustaceans

LIFE SPAN: Unknown

Velvet Belly Lanternshark

Etmopterus spinax

SAY IT! *"et-MOP-ter-us SPIH-nax"*

You might imagine that this shark feels soft, with a name like "velvet belly"! But this name actually comes from the color of the shark's belly, which is dark black. These small deep-sea sharks have photophores, which are small organs that give off light on their undersides. The light helps the shark blend in with light shining from the surface of the water. Scientists think that these sharks might also use their glowing bellies to send messages to each other!

SHARK STATS

COMMON NAME: Velvet belly lanternshark

SCIENTIFIC NAME: *Etmopterus spinax*

WHERE IT'S FOUND: Deep waters of Europe and western Africa

SIZE: Up to 18 inches

DIET: Small fish, squid, and shrimp

LIFE SPAN: Up to 20 years

Spiny Dogfish

Squalus acanthias

SAY IT! *"SKWAH-lus ah-KAN-thee-us"*

The name "spiny dogfish" gives us lots of clues about this fascinating shark. When spiny dogfish are bitten, the spines in their dorsal fins inject venom into the attacker. These sharks are also known to hunt in packs like dogs. Sometimes they hunt in packs of 1,000 sharks!

SHARK STATS

COMMON NAME: Spiny dogfish

SCIENTIFIC NAME: *Squalus acanthias*

WHERE IT'S FOUND: Shallow waters off the coasts of the eastern United States, South America, Europe, and Australia

SIZE: 3 to 4 feet

DIET: Fish, smaller sharks, octopus, squid, and crabs

LIFE SPAN: 20 to 24 years

Carcharhiniformes: Ground Sharks

Of all the shark orders, Carcharhiniformes, the ground sharks, is the largest. It contains more than 270 species that come in all sizes and shapes, including the unusual hammerhead sharks. Some species, like swell sharks and catsharks, hang out on the bottom. Others, like blue sharks and blacktip reef sharks, swim freely in open water.

To find the oldest members of this order, you'd have to go back more than 140 million years. That's when the earliest catsharks swam in ancient seas. Families in this order include weasel sharks, barbeled houndsharks, finback sharks, false catsharks, catsharks, requiem sharks, hammerhead sharks, and houndsharks.

What makes a ground shark a ground shark? They have five gill slits and nictitating eyelids. They also have two dorsal fins without spines, and anal fins. These sharks are found in almost every saltwater habitat, from areas near the coast to open ocean. Many species live in **estuaries**. An estuary is where an ocean and a river meet. A few sharks, like the Borneo river shark and the bull shark, swim into freshwater habitats like rivers. Many species are cold-blooded. This means their temperature is the same as the surrounding water. Others capture heat from their muscles to warm their bodies.

When it comes to having babies, these sharks reproduce in all three ways. Some species, like white sharks, give birth to as few as two pups after their eggs hatch inside the mother's body. Coral catsharks lay two eggs at a time. Blue sharks can give birth to as many as 100 pups in a single birthing!

Blue Shark

Prionace glauca

SAY IT! *"PRY-oh-nays GLAW-kah"*

Once the most plentiful shark in the ocean, this beautiful shark looks like a blue torpedo. Blue sharks eat fast and furiously—almost enough to burst. When they eat too much, the sharks may throw up, then start eating again. Fishermen call them "blue dogs" because they sometimes follow boats begging for scraps!

SHARK STATS

COMMON NAME: Blue shark

SCIENTIFIC NAME: *Prionace glauca*

WHERE IT'S FOUND: Temperate and tropical oceans worldwide, along continent edges in open water

SIZE: 10 to 13 feet

DIET: Fish, squid, cuttlefish, and small sharks

LIFE SPAN: Up to 20 years

Scalloped Hammerhead

Sphyrna lewini

SAY IT! *"SFUR-nuh loo-WEN-ee"*

Scalloped hammerheads live in large schools. They stay near the shore during the day, then swim farther out to hunt at night. All that time near the shore means that leeches and other parasites can latch on to them. In order to get rid of these pests, scalloped hammerheads visit "cleaning stations" in coral reefs, where small fish eat leeches off of their skin and out of their mouths.

SHARK STATS

COMMON NAME: Scalloped hammerhead

SCIENTIFIC NAME: *Sphyrna lewini*

WHERE IT'S FOUND: Warm, open oceans all around the world

SIZE: 7 to 11 feet

DIET: Fish, eels, squid, octopus, and rays

LIFE SPAN: 30 years

Leopard Shark

Triakis semifasciata

SAY IT! *"try-A-kis sim-ee-FASH-ee-AH-tuh"*

With its pretty black spots, the leopard shark might remind you of another hunter—its namesake, the leopard! This species of houndshark often travels with others of its kind in schools. Leopard sharks have overlapping teeth that form a flat surface. Called "pavement teeth," they are useful for crushing clams and crabs for supper!

SHARK STATS

COMMON NAME: Leopard shark

SCIENTIFIC NAME: *Triakis semifasciata*

WHERE IT'S FOUND: The Pacific Ocean, from Oregon, United States, to Mazatlán, Mexico; over sand, mud, and reefs near shore, and in estuaries down to 300 feet

SIZE: 48 inches to 7 feet

DIET: Crabs, clams, small fish, fish eggs, and worms

LIFE SPAN: Up to 30 years

Striped Catshark

Poroderma africanum

SAY IT! *"por-AH-der-mah af-rih-KAN-um"*

It's easy to identify this little shark. It looks like it's wearing striped pajamas! The striped catshark lurks in reef crevices during the day and hunts at night. Squid is one of this shark's favorite foods. The striped catshark sometimes hides among the squid's eggs, which are laid in "mats" on the bottom. Safely hidden, the shark snatches a mother squid as it is laying its eggs!

SHARK STATS

COMMON NAME: Striped shark or pajama shark

SCIENTIFIC NAME: *Poroderma africanum*

WHERE IT'S FOUND: Shallow water from 3 to 350 feet; limited to South Africa and Mauritius Island in the Indian Ocean

SIZE: 40 inches

DIET: Crabs, fish, and squid

LIFE SPAN: 12 to 13 years

Lamniformes: Mackerel Sharks

When most people think of a shark, the great white usually comes to mind. This shark belongs to the Lamniformes order, a group that includes some of the Earth's most dramatic sharks. Also called mackerel sharks, this order has 17 living species. The ancient megalodon belonged to this group, as does the fastest shark in the ocean—the speedy mako. It can swim in bursts up to 60 miles per hour, which is as fast as a car on the highway.

These sharks live in all the world's oceans at all different depths. Many species are strong swimmers and active predators in open water. Some scavenge along the bottom or live in the ocean's mysterious dark depths. The seven families of this order are mackerel sharks, thresher sharks, basking sharks, megamouth sharks, goblin sharks, sand sharks, and crocodile sharks. Although this group has many active hunters, it also includes two filter feeders, the megamouth and the basking shark.

Mackerel sharks have five gills, two dorsal fins, and an anal fin. They don't have nictitating eyelids and their mouths are located behind the front of their eyes. Their bodies come in different shapes—from short and thick to long and almost eel-like. Mackerel shark tails can be shaped like a great white's (top and bottom parts are the same size) or like a crocodile shark's (long upper part and small lower part).

These sharks are warm-blooded. They have a higher body temperature than the surrounding water. Being a baby mackerel shark is dangerous. The sharks that hatch first inside their mother may eat their siblings!

What about teeth? Fish eaters like the sand tigers have pointed teeth. Sharks like the great white that hunt mammals and big fish have large cutting teeth. **Filter feeders** like the megamouth and basking shark have tiny teeth.

Goblin Shark

Mitsukurina owstoni

SAY IT! *"mit-soo-koo-REE-nah ohs-TOH-nee"*

The goblin shark looks like a creepy villain from a fairy tale. With pink skin, a mouth full of needle-sharp teeth, and a long, pointy snout, this shark is a ferocious hunter. Its jaws can snap forward at six feet per second to snatch prey—faster than any other shark. The goblin shark looks pink, but the color is from blood vessels underneath its see-through skin.

SHARK STATS

COMMON NAME: Goblin shark

SCIENTIFIC NAME: *Mitsukurina owstoni*

WHERE IT'S FOUND: Temperate oceans in midwater to more than 4,250 feet deep; in parts of the Pacific, Atlantic, and around Australia

SIZE: 5 to 12.6 feet

DIET: Deepwater fish, crabs, octopuses, and squid

LIFE SPAN: Unknown, possibly 35 years

Megamouth Shark

Megachasma pelagios

SAY IT! *"meh-gah-KAS-mah peh-LA-jee-ohs"*

A megamouth shark's mega-sized mouth is big enough to hold a second grader, lying down. But don't worry! These gentle giants are **filter feeders**. Megamouths look like they are wearing white lipstick on their upper lip. Some scientists think this helps attract prey—right into the shark's mouth! These large sharks are rare. The first one was spotted in 1976 and only about 100 have been seen since.

SHARK STATS

COMMON NAME: Megamouth shark

SCIENTIFIC NAME: *Megachasma pelagios*

WHERE IT'S FOUND: Open ocean in upper water down to 15,000 feet; in all oceans, but most common off Japan, China, and the Philippines

SIZE: 17 feet

DIET: Krill, plankton, jellyfish

LIFE SPAN: Unknown, likely long-lived

Salmon Shark

Lamna ditropis

SAY IT! *"LAM-nah dye-TROH-pis"*

You might think that a salmon shark looks a lot like a great white shark; they are both mackerel sharks! The trick to telling the difference is the dark blotches that only salmon sharks have on their pale underbellies (white sharks don't have them). The salmon shark migrates long distances to raise their young in warm waters and, possibly, to follow fish like salmon, its favorite food.

SHARK STATS

COMMON NAME: Salmon shark

SCIENTIFIC NAME: *Lamna ditropis*

WHERE IT'S FOUND: Coastal waters of the North Pacific; Japan, North Korea, South Korea, Russia, Canada, and the United States; from surface to 500 feet

SIZE: Up to 10 feet

DIET: Bony fish like salmon; squid

LIFE SPAN: 20 to 27 years

Common Thresher Shark

Alopias vulpinus

SAY IT! *"ah-LOH-pee-us vul-PYE-nus"*

You've already read that thresher sharks whip their long tails at prey to stun it. These sharks also use their tails to leap out of the water. Some thresher sharks can leap 20 feet into the air while spinning around like a gymnast. This is called breaching and it may also help the thresher shark capture prey.

SHARK STATS

COMMON NAME: Thresher shark

SCIENTIFIC NAME: *Alopias vulpinus*

WHERE IT'S FOUND: Coastal and open ocean in tropical and temperate waters worldwide; from surface to 1,800 feet

SIZE: 25 feet

DIET: Schooling fish like mackerel, sardines, menhaden, and bonito

LIFE SPAN: Up to 50 years

Great White Shark

Carcharodon carcharias

SAY IT! *"kar-KAIR-uh-don kar-KAIR-ee-us"*

Great white sharks, which scientists and shark experts call white sharks, are the largest predatory sharks in the world. They can weigh 6,000 pounds or more. That is more than a large SUV! You might expect such a large animal to be slow, but great whites can swim up to 25 miles per hour in short bursts. Great whites are apex predators. This means they are at the top of the food chain, but once in a while an orca may kill a great white.

SHARK STATS

COMMON NAMES: Great white shark, white shark, white pointer

SCIENTIFIC NAME: *Carcharodon carcharias*

WHERE IT'S FOUND: Coastal and open tropical and temperate oceans; depths 0 to 5,000 feet

SIZE: 20 feet (possibly greater)

DIET: Seals, sea lions, dolphins, some whales

LIFE SPAN: 70 years

Hexanchiformes: Cow Sharks and Frilled Sharks

Do you want to meet some ancient sharks? Let me introduce you to the Hexanchiformes—also known as the cow sharks and the frill sharks. This order includes the sevengill sharks, sixgill sharks, and frilled sharks. These sharks are unique since they have six or seven pairs of gills and one dorsal fin, located far back on the body. Fossils of these sharks are about 170 million years old! There are six species alive today.

Frilled sharks are sometimes called living fossils because they look a lot like the prehistoric sharks did. They are long and skinny, almost like big eels. Their gills are large and flow in the water, which makes them look frilly. Frilled sharks live in open water and sometimes hang out in water 5,500 feet deep or more. Look inside a frilled shark's long, flexible jaws and you will find 300 sharp teeth in rows of three.

Cow sharks look very different from frilled sharks. They have thick bodies and large, teardrop-shaped eyes that are often green and adapted to see in low light. Their bodies are usually dark, and some have spots. Cow sharks spend most of their time in deep water and have been seen as deep as 6,150 feet. Like many other sharks, they sometimes migrate to shallower water to eat or breed. These sharks have a lot of babies at once. The broadnose sevengill may give birth to more than 100 babies at the same time!

Broadnose Sevengill Shark

Notorynchus cepedianus

SAY IT! *"noh-toh-REEN-kus seh-fih-dye-AY-nus"*

This large cow shark with its big, rounded snout and body looks a little like a blimp with black and white spots. Broadnose sevengills sometimes stalk their prey. They quietly approach from behind and strike at the last minute, surprising their catch. These sharks eat almost anything—including other sharks, dolphins, and seals.

SHARK STATS

COMMON NAME: Broadnose sevengill shark

SCIENTIFIC NAME: *Notorynchus cepedianus*

WHERE IT'S FOUND: All oceans except the North Atlantic; found along the continental shelf to 550 feet, including shallow bays and estuaries

SIZE: 10 feet

DIET: Small sharks, seals, fish, and dead animals

LIFE SPAN: 30 to 50 years

Bluntnose Sixgill Shark

Hexanchus griseus

SAY IT! *"hex-AN-kus GRIH-see-us"*

Looking at a bluntnose sixgill shark is like looking into the past. It has not changed much for 200 million years. These secretive creatures spend most of their time in very deep water, up to 8,000 feet. Sometimes divers in South Africa or the Olympic Sound will get lucky and see one of these big guys as they come up to feed in shallower water.

SHARK STATS

COMMON NAME: Bluntnose sixgill shark

SCIENTIFIC NAME: *Hexanchus griseus*

WHERE IT'S FOUND: All oceans in deep water, except the Antarctic, but also in bays

SIZE: 16 feet

DIET: Fish, rays, hagfish, ratfish, and dead animals

LIFE SPAN: 80 years

Sharpnose Sevengill

Heptranchias perlo

SAY IT! *"hep-TRAN-kee-us PER-loh"*

Can sharks smile? They can't, but the sharpnose sevengill swims with its mouth open, which makes it look like it's wearing a giant smile. This is another deepwater cow shark; it lives in water up to 3,000 feet deep. The sharpnose sevengill has big green eyes that seem to glow in the darker water.

SHARK STATS

COMMON NAME: Sharpnose sevengill

SCIENTIFIC NAME: *Heptranchias perlo*

WHERE IT'S FOUND: Oceans worldwide except the north Pacific, in deep water

SIZE: 4.6 feet

DIET: Small sharks, rays, bony fish, crabs, lobsters, and squid

LIFE SPAN: 50 years

Bigeyed Sixgill Shark

Hexanchus nakamurai

SAY IT! *"hex-AN-kus nah-kah-MOO-rye"*

Scientists believe that bigeyed sixgill sharks—so named for having six gill slits rather than the usual five that most sharks have—live all across the world. But these mysterious sharks are difficult to study because they inhabit such deep waters. The bigeyed sixgill has amazingly large eyes that shine a bright, reflective green to help them see in the dark as they hunt.

SHARK STATS

COMMON NAME: Bigeyed sixgill shark

SCIENTIFIC NAME: *Hexanchus nakamurai*

WHERE IT'S FOUND: In deep waters around the world

SIZE: 5 to 6 feet

DIET: Small fish, crabs

LIFE SPAN: Unknown

Orectolobiformes: Carpet Sharks

When you hear the nickname "carpet sharks," what pops into your head? Sharks as flat as pancakes? Sharks that are fuzzy? Many members of Orectolobiformes spend a lot of time on the ocean floor and have patterned skins that remind some people of fancy carpets. This is how they earned their nickname.

This order has about 43 species that look quite different from one another. It includes the giant whale shark, which is not only the largest shark but the largest fish in the sea. Blind sharks, nurse sharks, bamboo sharks, wobbegongs, collared carpet sharks, and zebra sharks are all members of this group. Orectolobiformes have been around since dinosaurs walked the earth more than 100 million years ago.

These sharks are very different from one another, but they do have some things in common. All carpet sharks have five gills, two dorsal fins, and an anal fin. Many, like the nurse shark, have fingerlike barbels on their chins. Some, like whale sharks, have mouths that are on the front of their head. Most, like the wobbegong, have mouths underneath. Most species have a tail fin that is nearly straight in line with the body and doesn't stick up. Many species do not need to swim to breathe and spend most of their time on the bottom.

These sharks stick to shallow and medium-deep warm water. Many species live in the tropical waters of the Indo-Pacific, but a couple patrol the Atlantic and Pacific oceans. Many species are nocturnal and hide under ledges and in caves during the day. Some carpet sharks lay egg cases, while others give birth to live pups.

Whale Shark

Rhincodon typus

SAY IT! *"RIN-koh-don TYE-fus"*

The largest fish in the sea eats some of the smallest animals—microscopic plankton and tiny krill. Whale sharks swim around with their mouths open to strain out these tiny creatures. These big boys are about 40 feet long, which is about as long as a school bus. But don't let their size scare you. These gentle giants don't mind when swimming humans come to say hello!

SHARK STATS

COMMON NAME: Whale shark

SCIENTIFIC NAME: *Rhincodon typus*

WHERE IT'S FOUND: All tropical and warm temperate seas, except the Mediterranean, from surface to 650 feet

SIZE: 40 to 60 feet

DIET: Plankton, krill, fish eggs, shrimp, and schooling fish

LIFE SPAN: 60 to 70 years

Epaulette Shark

Hemiscyllium ocellatum

SAY IT! *"him-ih-SIL-ee-um ah-sih-LAY-tum"*

Did you know some sharks can walk? The epaulette shark can! It uses its pectoral fins to walk along the ocean floor. If that isn't impressive enough, this little shark can even walk between tidal pools—leaving the water to do so! They can live for up to an hour without a good supply of oxygen.

SHARK STATS

COMMON NAME: Epaulette shark

SCIENTIFIC NAME: *Hemiscyllium ocellatum*

WHERE IT'S FOUND: Shallow water; northern coast of Australia and southern New Guinea

SIZE: 42 inches

DIET: Small fish and **invertebrates**

LIFE SPAN: 20 to 25 years

Tasseled Wobbegong

Eucrossorhinus dasypogon

SAY IT! *"yoo-kros-ih-RYE-nus DAS-ih-puh-gon"*

The tasseled wobbegong takes the name "carpet shark" very seriously. Not only does it have pretty patterns all over its body, it also has tassels like an Oriental rug! With camouflage this good, the wobbegong can hide in plain sight while it waits for dinner. To lure prey close, it may wiggle its tail, which looks like a small fish.

SHARK STATS

COMMON NAME: Tasseled wobbegong

SCIENTIFIC NAME: *Eucrossorhinus dasypogon*

WHERE IT'S FOUND: Western Pacific in Papua New Guinea and North Australia; on coral sand and rubble

SIZE: 4 feet

DIET: Bottom fish and invertebrates

LIFE SPAN: Unknown

Nurse Shark

Ginglymostoma cirratum

SAY IT! *"ging-lee-mohs-TOH-mus ser-RAH-tum"*

Nurse sharks really like being around other nurse sharks, especially during the day. Groups of 40 or more of these bottom-dwelling sharks huddle together in caves until nighttime. Nurse sharks use very strong suction to grab prey. They may get their name from the sucking sound they make when hunting.

SHARK STATS

COMMON NAME: Nurse shark

SCIENTIFIC NAME: *Ginglymostoma cirratum*

WHERE IT'S FOUND: Shallow bottoms and deeper reefs in the tropical Atlantic

SIZE: 8 feet

DIET: Fish, **mollusks**, crabs, and snails

LIFE SPAN: 15 to 20 years

Zebra Shark

Stegostoma fasciatum

SAY IT! *"steg-ah-STOH-mah fash-ee-AY-tum"*

If this animal is called a zebra shark, why does it have spots like a leopard? Good question! When the pups are born, they have black and white or yellow stripes. As they grow into adults, the stripes become spots. Like nurse sharks, zebra sharks have strong jaw muscles that let them suck fish right out of their hiding places.

SHARK STATS

COMMON NAME: Zebra shark

SCIENTIFIC NAME: *Stegostoma fasciatum*

WHERE IT'S FOUND: Tropical water in the western and eastern Indian Ocean

SIZE: 8 feet

DIET: Mollusks, crabs, and small fish

LIFE SPAN: 25 years

Heterodontiformes: Bullhead Sharks

Which sharks have a snout like a pig, spines on their dorsal fins, and a ridge that looks like eyebrows? They are the bottom-dwelling Heterodontiformes, also known as bullhead sharks. The nine species of sharks in this group are on the smaller side. The largest species is just five feet long. They like the warm areas of the Atlantic, Pacific, and Indian oceans. All species live on the bottom in coral reefs, in rocky reefs, and on soft kelp beds. Members of this order started swimming the oceans 200 million years ago.

Let's talk about the bullhead sharks' most interesting features. These sharks have a piglike snout and a very good sense of smell. Look inside a bullhead shark's mouth and you will notice that their front teeth are sharp and their back teeth are flat, like molars. The flat teeth are perfect for crushing clams, crabs, and other prey with hard shells. The name Heterodontiformes means "different teeth." These guys also have a hard ridge above each eye. This is what makes them look like they have a face like a bull.

Bullhead sharks stay mostly in shallow water up to 300 feet. They are nocturnal and hunt at night. These sharks can't swim very well and look clumsy while doing it, but at least they are pretty! Sharks in this order have unique colorful spots, stripes, and blotches. This camouflage is perfect for helping them hide from predators like sevengill sharks and sea lions.

Heterodontiformes lay eggs. Their egg cases are amazing spiral shapes that look like thick screws. The mother shark takes her screw-shaped cases and wedges them into little spaces. The cases are usually so tightly wedged that predators give up before they are able to pull them free.

Port Jackson Shark

Heterodontus portusjacksoni

SAY IT! *"heh-ter-oh-DON-tus por-tus-jak-SOH-nee"*

Also known as an oyster crusher, the Port Jackson shark is named after a port in Australia. While many sharks eat their food whole, this shark seems to grind its hard-shelled food with its flat teeth before swallowing it. Port Jackson sharks have a good memory and good sense of location. They often return to the same sites every year to lay their eggs.

SHARK STATS

COMMON NAME: Port Jackson shark	**SIZE:** 5.5 feet
SCIENTIFIC NAME: *Heterodontus portusjacksoni*	**DIET:** Small fish, crabs, and mollusks
WHERE IT'S FOUND: Temperate waters around the southern coast of Australia	**LIFE SPAN:** 30 years

Pacific Horn Shark

Heterodontus francisci

SAY IT! *"heh-ter-oh-DON-tus fran-SIS-see"*

Sometimes it's easier to crawl than swim when you are a bullhead shark! Pacific horn sharks have strong pelvic and ventral fins that they use to "crawl" along the bottom. This species hunts octopuses and crabs but especially loves spiny sea urchins. Sometimes this shark's teeth turn brown from eating them!

SHARK STATS

COMMON NAME: Pacific horn shark

SCIENTIFIC NAME: *Heterodontus francisci*

WHERE IT'S FOUND: Continental shelf off California, Pacific Ocean

SIZE: 4.1 feet

DIET: Sea urchins, anemones, mollusks, octopuses, and crabs

LIFE SPAN: 25 years

Zebra Bullhead

Heterodontus zebra

SAY IT! *"heh-ter-oh-DON-tus ZEE-brah"*

This bottom-dwelling shark has beautiful zebra-like stripes along its body, helping it to blend in with the play of light from the ocean surface above. Usually these sharks prefer shallow waters, but the zebra bullheads near Australia swim deeper, and have been found in waters up to 650 feet deep.

SHARK STATS

COMMON NAME: Zebra bullhead

SCIENTIFIC NAME: *Heterodontus zebra*

WHERE IT'S FOUND: Shallow waters off the coasts of Japan, China, Vietnam, Indonesia, and Australia

SIZE: 4 feet

DIET: Shellfish, clams, urchins, and small fish

LIFE SPAN: Unknown

Galápagos Bullhead Shark

Heterodontus quoyi

SAY IT! *"heh-ter-oh-DON-tus KWOH-yee"*

This shark looks like it is covered in dark brown polka dots. Even its fins have spots! Although real catsharks are part of the ground shark order, Galápagos bullheads are sometimes called "cat sharks" because their eyes look like a cat's. It lives in the waters around the Galápagos Islands, and off the coast of South America near south Ecuador and Peru.

SHARK STATS

COMMON NAME: Galápagos bullhead shark

SCIENTIFIC NAME: *Heterodontus quoyi*

WHERE IT'S FOUND: Shallow water to 130 feet; eastern Pacific and Galápagos Islands

SIZE: 42 inches

DIET: Mollusks, crabs, and invertebrates

LIFE SPAN: Unknown

Japanese Bullhead Shark

Heterodontus japonicus

SAY IT! *"heh-ter-oh-DON-tus jah-PON-ih-kus"*

Let's face it. Shark mothers aren't the best, but the Japanese bullhead perhaps tries a little harder than most to ensure her babies survive. Females sometimes lay their egg cases in nests shared with other females. This may help their babies survive, since there is safety in numbers. The eggs take about a year to hatch.

SHARK STATS

COMMON NAME: Japanese bullhead shark

SCIENTIFIC NAME: *Heterodontus japonicus*

WHERE IT'S FOUND: Rocky reefs and kelp forests, down to 90 feet; along the coast of China

SIZE: Up to 4 feet

DIET: Small fish, crustaceans, and mollusks

LIFE SPAN: Unknown

Great white shark

CONCLUSION

I hope, after reading this book, that you are as excited about sharks as I am. I also hope you will keep exploring and learning more about these fantastic creatures. Sharks have survived for hundreds of millions of years, but now they are in danger. Some species are at risk of disappearing forever. When we see sharks, that is a good sign that their ocean home is healthy. Don't be scared if you see one!

What can you do to help? Try to eat seafood that is caught in a responsible way. Volunteer for a beach cleanup. When plastic ends up in the ocean, it hurts not only sharks but many ocean animals. At home, try to use reusable containers and bottles instead of plastics you use once and throw away.

Excitement is contagious! Discuss threats to sharks and marine life at your school and share this book with your friends. All life is important, and together we will keep sharks—and the oceans—safe for all of us.

MORE TO EXPLORE

BOOKS

If Sharks Disappeared by Lily Williams

Neighborhood Sharks by Katherine Roy

Shark Lady by Jess Keating

Smart About Sharks! by Owen Davey

Swimming with Sharks by Heather Lang

The Ultimate Shark Book for Kids by Jenny Kellett

CONSERVATION ORGANIZATIONS

oceana.org

sharkstewards.org

LIVE WEBCAMS

MONTEREY BAY AQUARIUM:
montereybayaquarium.org

AQUARIUM OF THE PACIFIC:
aquariumofpacific.org

WEBSITES

FLORIDA MUSEUM:
floridamuseum.ufl.edu/discover-fish

REEFQUEST CENTRE FOR SHARK RESEARCH:
elasmo-research.org

MONTEREY BAY AQUARIUM:
montereybayaquarium.org

GLOSSARY

AMBUSH PREDATION: a way of hunting where an animal quietly waits for prey, then attacks when it comes close

AMPULLAE OF LORENZINI: special organs on sharks' snouts that can detect tiny electrical signals

BARBELS: dangling, fleshy "whiskers" on a shark's snout or chin that are used to sense prey

BENTHIC: living at, or being near, the bottom of the ocean

CARTILAGINOUS FISH: fish that have skeletons made of cartilage instead of bone

CONTINENTAL SHELF: the steep slope under the ocean that forms a continent's border

DERMAL DENTICLE: toothlike scales on a shark's skin

ELECTRORECEPTION: the ability to detect electrical signals

ESTUARY: where an ocean and a river meet

EVOLVE: to change slowly over time

EXTINCT: when a living thing no longer exists anywhere on Earth

FILTER FEEDER: an animal that eats by filtering tiny food particles from the water

FOSSIL: a print or parts of prehistoric plants or animals left in stone

HABITAT: where an animal or insect lives

INVERTEBRATES: animals without backbones, such as insects, crustaceans, worms, mollusks, jellyfish, starfish, and many others

LATERAL LINE: a line on the sides of a fish with sense organs that detect pressure and vibration

MIGRATE: to move from one area to another for food or to breed

MOLLUSKS: invertebrate animals like snails, slugs, mussels, and octopuses with soft bodies; many have shells

NICTITATING MEMBRANE: a third eyelid that is clear and protects the eye while a shark feeds

PHEROMONE: a chemical made by an animal to communicate with others of its species

PREDATOR: an animal that hunts other animals to eat

PREY: an animal that is hunted by another animal for food

SPECIES: a group of living beings that have many things in common and can mate to make others of their kind

SPIRACLES: a pair of holes just behind the eyes that suck water in and push it past the gills

TAXONOMY: a scientific system used to describe and name every living thing on Earth

TEMPERATE: an area that is not too hot or too cold

TROPICAL: an area that is warm all the time

INDEX

H

I

J

K

L

M

N

O

P

ACKNOWLEDGMENTS

I would like to thank all the teachers and professors who have inspired me to learn about the oceans, and the students I have inspired and who have continued to inspire me to learn, to share, and to grow. Without the love and support of my family, most of all my mother, I would not have been given the education and the support to learn and to teach.

Dr. John McCosker has been a leader in research and a champion for sharks, and I am ever grateful to have worked with him at the California Academy of Sciences. As a shark conservationist with Shark Stewards, I would not be able to continue our work saving sharks without the daily contributions of volunteers who are passionate about shark protection and ocean health, and the donors and funders that support our organization.

I am grateful to my friends and scuba divers in Singapore, Borneo, Malaysia, Indonesia, and Timor-Leste who are working with us to better understand and save sharks. It is easy to blame others who are different from us, so I give thanks to Dr. Vincent Yip, our student Alice, and her parents, Mr. and Mrs. Zhao, for showing me China and giving me a great appreciation for a deep and rich culture. They allowed us to work to help educate that culture on the importance of saving sharks by avoiding shark fin soup, and to do so with empathy.

I would like to thank the editors at Callisto Media for publishing this book, and most of all, the young readers who will help to save sharks and keep the ocean healthy!

ABOUT THE AUTHOR

DAVID McGUIRE is the founder and director of the nonprofit Shark Stewards, whose mission is to restore ocean health by saving sharks and protecting critical marine habitat. A marine biologist, David holds a master's degree in environmental health from University of California at Berkeley. David is the writer, producer, and underwater cinematographer of several award-winning documentaries, including an Emmy Award–winning series on a Philippines biodiversity expedition called *Reefs to Rainforests*.

A sailor and diver, David has participated in several ocean expeditions around the world for National Geographic and the California Academy of Sciences, where he is a research associate. He has also published numerous articles on the state of the ocean and sharks, and writes a blog on sharks and ocean health for *National Geographic*. He is a popular public speaker on sharks and the ocean; lectures at several universities, including UC Berkeley; and is an adjunct professor at the University of San Francisco.